WELCOME!

WELCOME!

Poems
by

THOMAS SHAPCOTT

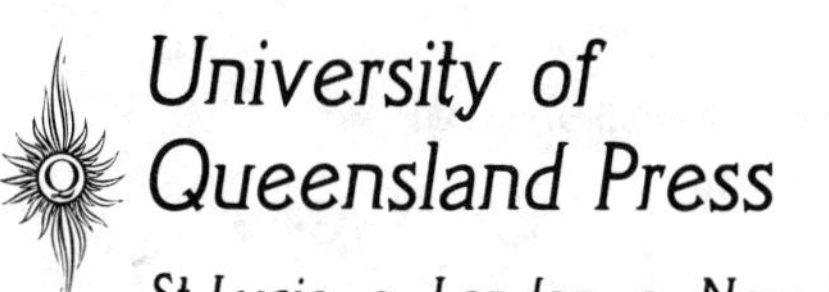

University of
Queensland Press

St Lucia ● London ● New York

University of Queensland Press, St Lucia, Queensland 1983
© Thomas W. Shapcott

This book is copyright. Apart from any fair dealing for the
purposes of private study, research, criticism, or review, as
permitted under the Copyright Act, no part may be reproduced
by any process without written permission. Enquiries should be
made to the publishers.

Typeset by University of Queensland Press
Printed and bound by Richard Clay (S.E.Asia) Pte Ltd, Singapore

Distributed in the United Kingdom, Europe, the Middle East,
Africa, and the Caribbean by Prentice-Hall International,
International Book Distributors Ltd, 66 Wood Lane End, Hemel
Hempstead, Herts., England.

Published with the assistance of the Literature Board
of the Australia Council

National Library of Australia
Cataloguing-in-Publication data

Shapcott, Thomas W. (Thomas William), 1935–
    Welcome!

    ISBN 0 7022 1922 3.
    ISBN 0 7022 1932 0 (pbk.).

    I. Title.

A821'.3

Library of Congress Cataloging in Publication Data

Shapcott, Thomas W.
    Welcome! : poems.

    I. Title.
PR9619.3.S47W4   1983   821   83–5857
ISBN 0-7022-1922-3
ISBN 0-7022-1032-0 (pbk.)

For Judith and David

Acknowledgments

To the Literature Board of the Australia Council for Senior Writing Fellowship during which most of these poems were written.

To Kelvin Grove College of Advanced Education (Brisbane), the Western Australian Institute of Technology (Perth), Deakin University (Victoria), Riverina College of Advanced Education, Darling Downs Institute of Advanced Education and Adelaide University for terms as Writer In Residence, during which this manuscript achieved its present form.

To Judith Rodriguez and David Malouf, whose advice on matters of selection and final polishing of poems was invaluable.

To Coach House Press, Toronto, Canada, for booklet published in their MS Editions Series to coincide with International Writers' Week at Harbourfront Readings, Toronto 1980, and to the following papers and journals for first publication of individual poems: *The Age, Ariel* (Canada), *Artlook, The Australian, The Border Issue, The Bulletin, Canberra Times, The Courier Mail, Compass, Contempa, Fling, Helix, Kunapipi* (Denmark), *The Literary Review* (Edinburgh), *Makar, Mattoid, Meanjin, New Letters* (USA), *New Poetry, Northern Light* (Canada), *Overland, Poetry Australia, Prism International* (Canada), *Quadrant, Semper, Southerly, Sydney Morning Herald, Tasmanian Review, The Last Poets Choice, Waves* (Canada), *Westerly.*

Contents

The Eel Teller

"Can't kill 'em. Other night
I caught this eel down
by that pool, that one, we
call it the skullhole.
Chopped off its head, slit
and gutted it. The bastard
soaked in a tub of brine
till beer-time.
Then I tossed it in a bag,
bottom of the fridge. An hour later
it tried to get back out.
Can't kill 'em."

Leaning against this kitchen chair
he rips off another lager cap
while we pick his brains
for more. The meat boils up
against the saucepan lid, waiting.
"Was it the Tolai tribes", I ask aloud,
"who'd gulp the throbbing brains of enemies
to gain their souls?" No one remembers.
"That's a bit far-fetched". He serves
the pale flesh to us. Deeps
of the Shoalhaven flash
like a reflex. We hoe in.

Walking in circles, Canada

There was the time out on the Nullabor
when we realized bluebush had wiped out
all traces of the dirt track. I looked up
at flat sky, appalled. Not even wind-trees
could identify place. A cloud over the sun
and direction vanishes.

Now, pushing through autumn tangles of Canadian bush
thick underfelt-footed, gold, crackling out moisture
with swamp rumours, our footprints are rubbed out
by peatbog. We see horizontal. We remain vertical.
We return to log-rot quizzed fifteen minutes before.
Rain overhang, leaf overhang, branch cording them tight —
everything repeated. You promised us
the confidence of old logger's tracks
but we are in this together, lost, European
as the idea of the circle.

Exorcising ghosts and ancestors

I
In a hire car I seek out SHAPCOTT BARTON
the farmhouse-manor from before Norman times.
What does it reveal of those Shapcots, Shapcotes,
big in Exeter
then ekeing out village inheritances?
Souvenir fields, damp hills clamping the horizon
onto a straggle of stolid buildings. I skid
in the shuffle of cow dung, the reek of damp rust
exposes bony machinery. Not any garden.
II
When I was two I could not speak my own name.
At twelve I was spelling it right, the first line
of a ladder that ended "The World, The Universe".
At twenty-two not even my father understood,
my name was a waiting-room. Thirty-two
and I observed how my own children shuffled the Tarot Pack
of ancestors, slapping down profiles.
I am forty-two. Sequence confirms
genetic conspiracy.
III
Thomas Shapcotts link into vertebrae, the nerve source travels
five hundred years. Further.
We are never sure what we are becoming, though the texture
I observe in neighbour Devon faces settles me right enough
— I, who would wish myself fine-boned, sensitive, unique.

IV
Stooped lanes beneath hedges —
even fifty years back this would seize-up in bad weather.
Beyond that the mind lets in slowly
true isolation, a grip remote from villages.
That tradition of restlessness.
V
Checking ancient registers. "The old buildings",
the rector remarks companionably, "are cold, not a little
        unpleasant
— designed to 'put down enthusiasm' as they used to say."
1684, 1704: three or four marriages a year, twenty births,
as many deaths. Years repeat pattern before change. I sit
in the uneven (Saxon to Tudor) vestry, taking notes.
And still the uncanny shock: handwriting scripted my name
three hundred years back.
VI
My father died in 1972
five years later his four sons
began to stretch separate ways.
We were a close uncomfortable family.
VII
Last week in Bath
I saw the remains of a Roman pavement
unearthed in the Hospital foundations.
The stepson of the oldest known Shapcote
was the first Earl of Bath. My grandfather
when he retired in 1925 was on 25/- a week.
Through the Devon hills whole settlements vanish.
Traceworks of startled ages linger, embedded,
are uncovered. We are puzzled at our own feeling of awe,
at our own ordinariness.

Digging up a well

The afternoon to uncover that old well.
Under rubble of concrete, we shape
handclasps of unmorticed brick,
a circle eight feet wide treading its wall
through clay to a depth
that grunts

                      1972 in Exeter I was pacing
                      the Cathedral flagstone for
                      Thomas Shapcote Esq. Master
                      Extraordinary for the Chancellor's
                      Court Anno Domine 1660: onetime
                      "peculiar friend" of Herrick.
                      Outside, excavations to a Roman
                      Temple: an unearthed layer of bones
                      mass grave of unrecorded plague,
                      revolt, a whole village

      cat
      once buried cat
      lovely puss who sat
      face close
      to nibble earlobe-nipple
      (remember that)
      this is her skull look
      cat fluffcat look at
      that
                all those hill fossils
                in our backyard as kids
                stubbing toes on carbon fern
                trees dried into alphabet traces
                baked inscriptions in the split shale
                of my father's carrot bed

digging up a well
determined
to break fingernails
to unfold layers of
                         Why not say it:
                         we dig for gods'
                         shards; bones, something
                         once fondled
                  as if we did not have
                  the only power, now, to touch
                  to reach out, wrench
                  or be fully ripe
            Gods of fossil   glass gods   bones
            crockery kitchen gods in mass burials
            sacred cats
the whole widens
yes afternoon does darken
we have been foretold
but we are here
simple as that
            we sit on the rim
            uncovered
                  drinking beer
                  something rippling us
                  something through us looking
                  at us
                         breaking the ribs like petals
                         having a dry breath
                         so light we hardly notice
                         the sun is not our wristwatch
and that the discovered well
does not matter. We have opened
something. Another beer? Quick,
a photograph, here, by the
opened well. Hold it.

The Chesterfield in the wheat

Because I did not see the old chair
undone among sheep in the stubble
like old fleece on a thornbush
I am left with its absence
in every field I drive past
as if some flawed scarecrow were leaning
behind to point *now, now,* waiting to let go my shadow
and set up its hessian shanty again and to sing
loud worksongs to silence.
It will become litter among sheep.
It will loll back witless
at true glare. It will be accepted.
Only then I will be driving fast
and not looking, nothing needed, I will be
imprinted
onto the car's vinyl
as if it were my grandfather's chesterfield
as if the paddocks were empty.

Silence

"I suggest there comes a point in one's life when silence is called
for."   Fay Zwicky, radio interview 20.9.1979

I
As if we should have been engineered for
silence
we cry out in the very act of birth
to express anger at our pulse
we cram head and shoulder through
lips
to the cavern. Darkness supposes us
already full-grip, toes splayed
in ironcap boots, terrestrial.
Air holds us now
entirely within its opening.
No sound of lips.
No closing.
II
Smetana in his dream of deafness
envied Beethoven the sanity
of no hearing. He himself,
jabbed by a long high A,
turned sound to a silence
aching with yellow teeth.
III
"But having conceived of it,
man must bring it to be."
Here on the sand floor
well in from the shaft
skeletal friction fondles our clothes.

Breath takes our time. The urge
is to tap messages, move the walls back.
They close in. Silence
is the dream that earth
is immobile. The earth is a body,
settling.
IV
"Space is a vast silence." Space is the tuning-board
of energy, meteor displacement, pizzicato.
Silence may be called for but the music
of the spheres has unheard pitch — is that
the same? Louis Jullien told Berlioz
it was perfect A, the terrestrial globe
revolving in space in his ear, God
as a blue cloud.
Whatever we dream, it is not silence.
Whatever we call for, it has a body.
V
Spliced by word strands
the rope jerks, a conjurer's trick
heading upward. Out of this basket
snake music
turns out the whole cave
like a pocket
full of clicking stones.
Fossils remember motion.
Inside those stern boots
someone's toes are tapping.
We have designs against time,
but that is to say
we have conceived of God.
Who holds us
in his mouth, considering.

Antignon creeper

Creepers are inhabiting you
they are dream zigzags
and will cover whole pages
— say while you are waiting
on that long phonecall
or looking out for the postman.
Outside, the fence sags
the silky-oak smothers
it is a clothespeg. Antignon
is restless as anxiety scribbling.
It smooths out shrubs, grasses,
fence and trees like a child's
hand. It dreams banquets
eight hundred guests seated
alfresco: late summer
and suddenly tendrils
reach out become flowers
festivals of crepe pink
and you on the point
of ripping everything down . . .

Acknowledging stormwater gutters
                            for Gwen Harwood

The hills of Brisbane invented us. Gutters that unplug
storm rain into hooping whooping cut-corner energy
invent rain to scald asphalt. That rain is you and me.
Heat takes this up, forced into the summer tug
of rain's war. In my Brisbane memories rain's the key to jog
the feel of what used to be.
                            We have moved elsewhere, free
once we invent ourselves.
                            But that summer swelter trapped me
once, in a crowd. Sweat soaked me: brow, chest, leg.
I wanted to rush outside, drench in rain. How forget
what childhood drummed into us, half the world and life away?
Somewhere we hoard the rush of stormwater gutters, toes direct
        spray
like punishment. It is not us any more. Free souls are a sad lot.
Yet to be invented by particular childhoods should be
born of the power of invention. Each of us invents necessity.

Ficus Benjaminii

Potted, behind a sofa in Stockholm.
On a Toronto platform, pruned.
Stephan Dom Vienna, and Ficus Benjaminii
swaying above tribute garlands, safe
in its tub.
Ficus Benjaminii takes something away
it deflects light deep into itself
a shady undercurrent of ripples
each leaf with its edge of ripples
dreaming of dampness, compost, humid
Queensland summer.

Ficus Benjaminii is mine.
The original tree claims my backyard,
children growing up share figtree shade
that foresaw their space four hundred years
and knotted its trunk to a giant's wrist
sinews two children cannot grip around.
They twitch in dreams for such security
the cubbyhouse ten feet up   no sun
a summer room of green benches beyond storms
never drought nothing disturbing spiders
that shall be harmless for life like the work of birds.
At night fruitbats weave charms to net stars,
beetles are brought blindfold, chubby slaves
that bump giggling caught in a grandfather tickle
the fig dreaming us there
                              we toss above damp sheets
and return alone, find the secrets, centuries
knotted in those wrists plunging through compost
under the falling hair of leaves that still ripple
like summer water when the sun slaps loud outside.

In my knuckles there is the remembrance of compost
there are green shoulders of leaves where you leave a shadow.
Stockholm, Vienna, Toronto: there are no spiders.
Ficus Benjaminii, indoors, trimmed for tubs,
we call it Weeping Fig in my country. You have
my birth legacy in your potplants
but only the rootless exile of its name.

Rehearsing the Ouija

What did we expect? We were in just that year
to expect anything (except, perhaps, the unexpected):
a clutter that had made, and performed,
its own opera and was gulping for more, loud for it.
A fortnight beach camp, then, for brain-storming
voice-scaring, high tuned encounters (there were many);
we were on the grape diet (your eyes will clear),
we went surfing, racing, we were discovering tensions
and each other. We planned the new performance.
One night someone suggested the Ouija. Cut out
paper alphabet, numerals, find an old wineglass.
We were instructed (who remembered?) to rest a finger,
lightly, each. The glass moved.
Nonsense strings of letters. Someone called out,
invoking the Presence.
                    I was drowsy (ideas
were encounters) I had to rest. Later, one of the lads
came in, electric. "Tom, it's a dead man,
he's telling his life."
                    The glass shuddered,
expelling words: "He was a Cedar getter",
they scrambled out history — wild cedar country,
1860. *He* ordered, *he* would lead. Hold
onto the rim. It was outside, up there, otherwise
no rest.
A silly bundle, children in their 20s (some older: me),
we reached in, fingers sustaining, somehow, thin glass.
We stumbled into May darkness. Cold, black electricity
kept stars in their distance, spiky. The girls
winced with giggles, we rippled — what possible harm?

We were so many. Up the rough path. Higher, shoving now
among bushes. Suddenly the glass split between us.
Quarry's edge. It was the old precipice.
That was the last time together. In rehearsal, later,
the new opera shattered. What did we expect?
Daytime we had all seen that fall. Someone called out,
invoking the Presence, forgetting its other name:
Absence.

for Robert Juniper

I The old grasstrees

Think of music. Think of music hunched
into a chord. The monody has hunched
into branches, slow, late. Think of sound
alone, before branches. Out there
in the place of the sky that stretches a long way
in the place of grass fidgeting
many notes one after another
out in that country of grasstrees
think back to music as one note.
Which note do you remember? And the next?
Think of the surprise of that first note,
the moment long before any grasstree remembers
you try to think of that. Nobody remembers
one note.
When the grasstree breaks into a chord
and we try to remember the first sounding together
two notes, three notes,
that is when the place of grasstrees instructs us.
Before we were here
before we brought the names for sound
grass-trees hunched, making not listening,
they were spreading the sky that stretches a long way
they were drinking the wind up
one note one note one note
they were coiling energy in layers
they were licking salt

and the moisture that sometimes comes with the wind.
Deep in their coils they were inventing the circle, music.
We came. We heard the remembering,
the surprise of that first note, and the next.
When we came into the place of grasstrees we marvelled
and leaned on our axes a moment.

II Seeds

They say
the spikes of grasstrees
open the stars.
Many buds
open along the shaft,
stars.
You have been surprised
each time.
Silence is always a surprise.
Sound surprises.
You have been watched, looking.
You have been opened, like a star.
Nothing you have known
opens the stars. Spikes
of grasstrees open.
You were wrong: nothing
is forbidden.

III Bushfire grasstrees

Song of black.
Song of something like black.
Song of blackened grasstrees after fire.
Song of grasstrees burned hard, biting hard
to be still gripping. Grasstrees toothless
biting into a sharp blue morning. Black gums
of grasstrees, stumps in a broken mouth.
Blue morning, sharp as if it could be yesterday.
Blue morning sharp as salt, sharp as frost sting.
As if it were yesterday.
As if yesterday were the same as this sharp blue morning.
Yesterday was the same morning, blue, salt sting biting.
The afternoon of bushfire, done in an hour, done
in half an hour, ten minutes. Not the waiting,
the waiting hunched into its one place, without time,
too busy concentrating, waiting. The time of waiting
was feel, place, immediate location. The grasstree
opens its blackened mouth to the blue morning. The event
is over, the waiting is over, there is only salt blue
of morning. Song of grasstrees, blackened, gripping
to bite, swallow, gulp pieces of blue morning.
Song of something like black, something like knowing
that again it is morning.

Parken Pregan Lagoon: Wagga Wagga

for John Olsen

I
Ponds of dry morning,
pockets of thistle scruff:
in Parken Pregan Lagoon the idea of water
is a tongue shoved into dust.
The idea of taste washes thought out.
To drink at Parken Pregan
close your eyes.
The Murrumbidgee is close:
think tight, squat down.

II
A knife sharpening stubble.
Take the wind out of your ears,
lick its sound quick
before it cuts. Taste
should be our most acute sense.

III
We have such belief in water,
it is ninety percent of ourself. Dry stubble
thistles burnt restless with summer —
when we have oiled their bodies
our children romp out, golden. Look away.
Dry lips, that your tongue
must now moisten.

IV
In our dream we have knelt down
in our richest place we have kept open
more than enough pause
to rustle like an avenue of poplars
at one instant. We planted well
there, it was a dream that gave shape
to the sunshine. Parken Pregan
was a limb that rolled over
out of the Murrumbidgee
shaking itself dry,
glistening.

V
The tongue, having first
tasted earth, waits
for its own moistening.
The lagoon is a dream
with its tongue lolling,
a brown creature under trees
dozing.

VI
When we wake, we are like ponds.
The summer voiced children, are they listening?
We hear it too. It is the change. When will it happen?

Mrs Midnight

"Custard-apple? What is that?
Can there be such a thing in nature?
Who would wish such a thing?"

The tree in my country grows to mature size
in backyards. That is, you must be prepared to sprawl,
duck under old clotheslines pegged out to any available corner
and keep an eye for bones.
The trees? They are not high.
They sprawl with knuckly branches,
with foliage like wide green lips.

Mrs Midnight wasn't at the party
Mrs Midnight picking her teeth
Mrs Midnight not invited
Mrs Midnight greasymouth hey Mrs Midnight
hey hey
picking skin squeezing skin tight as knuckles
calling for fruit

Custard-apples, ripe, are the size of two hands cupped out
only bigger. Their outer skin is thin and nobbled,
your knuckles. Imagine green knuckles
covering a fruit the size of your heart
barnacle knuckles
green
suspended
but of course everything else is different.

Mrs Midnight is up at table now watch her
she fiddles with rice spilling it
she smears butter with a bare fingerlick
snail trail now onto your silver

The inside of custard-apple is white
no, it is a thick-milk distortion
twine-bleached, fibrous. The inside
is a nest of compartments it tastes
like egg-clusters soft then sandy
you realize how smooth your tongue
sucks off the pulp.
Your mouth is a hard glossy seed.
Taste of sweetness has been told.
There was dryness, it had
colour of underground before the sun
forced it up into open juice. Softness
was once without lips.

Mrs Midnight is under the table
tasting sand.
Mrs Midnight flicks brown shiny seeds
something might grow
between toenail and itch
custard-apple trees
open their mouths.
Poor Mrs Midnight under the table
up here we are lined up
for fruit. Menu. Menu. Menu.

Spoon in and scoop. Taste.
Tongues lose colour
throats roll into corners
ten thousand eggshapes dissolve
unpolished marble
you are at sweet pith.

Fruitstalls are not friends.
This fruit must be always a gift.
Its origin is distant. Annona Cherimola:
Custard-apple is the name we have given it
as an act of possession.

Mrs Midnight has a rough tongue
Mrs Midnight red tongue
Mrs Midnight is licking the plates
Mrs Midnight will be joining the conversation
she insists on clacking your coffeespoon
she runs her eye along the rim
she has lodged something between your teeth
sandy. You hesitate. Mrs Midnight
she has songs what was it
backyard
you used bones for a drum
I used a tinful of seeds
spat-out custard-apple seeds
half grown we spat unformed eggsacs of pulp
we brought forth dry centres not salt not sodden
but so midnight-dry taste swelled to dirt
sandy   the grey core dissolved juice to bile
Mrs Midnight drew her knuckles up under your eyes
my fingernails stared back it's a grin

Now return to the soft ripe fruit. Begin.

The Toes

I
It is thought the big toe was once a claw.
It is a hinge. It is the doorway thrusting
us out into the world ready or not, accosting
brute fact of mud, gibber, dinosaur
trail or the spatter of cattlepat. Here
we are, out on our own, big toe pushing
down bracing, tensing, flexing
the strain up the ankle. The calf knots there
and into the groin — On your feet! Secure
all hatches for Upright Positions; the big toe has sent
its signals, body's tight and obedient.
Quick March Stop (Keep file. Dismiss). Before
troops slouch back to their beds they salute.
At night the toe jarrs like a warped door, last to be quiet.

II
The small toes splay when we take off that warm sock.
They stretch up, they curl down like children
wanting to dive into sandy water. The air's good enough then.
The small toes believe themselves dragons, they seek shock
and there is no way their size will contain them. Look
for yourself: are they part of you really? And to think everyone
has the same problem. Let them wear socks! Down
with the ambition of toes! Their place is to be constantly meek.

Imagine a world of toe independence. The mockery
of it — who could take seriously that runt little toe?
Impossible to give it ambition to flex and to grow
into what it might seem: claws indeed. They could rake
up the flesh of the leg, Tamurlaines under the sheet.
Some things children don't dream of. There are some things
                    children forget.

Brisbane in history

"The ghosts are leaving for Australia also"
Peter Redgrove: *A Thaw*

I
Say I dreamed it. Three priests and three
old women (one of them blind) standing to sing hymns
in that same park where the first church service
in Moreton Bay assembled. The ghost convicts
dragging their manacles sang *amen.* Their gaolers
shoved forward at the noise, then struck down
with muskets and chains and a group of Queensland police
wrenched at the singers. The blind woman stumbled
nearly to the ground. They were arrested for their song.
A sharp panic at the obedient officers brutalized
my anger.
The ghostly prisoners jeered and spat.
Their guards gave the burly police a wink.
The dream continues. It has the logic of madness.

1978

II
A ghost, you said, does not exist unless you see it.
In Australia they arrive, numbered; they are given
assignments.
They have never been told silence is the gaoler.
Australia was peopled by ghosts. They died
to create silence. Think of the death of ghosts:
a hundred years and no one looks backward.
Think of the very end of ghosts. That silence.
Ghosts brought agonies well enough
memories also, backward looks,
they kicked, screamed, loud echoes ripped

off their bodies. They knew their own suffering —
They believed in it, at the end.
They believed in lessons. Someone would learn.

The place of the triangle is now Wallace Bishop The Watch
        Specialist.
The first graveyard became the Roma Street Markets is now a
        Parking Lot.
The Tower Mill means a motel vantage point above the Logan
        Treadmill
(National Trust). There are no ghosts rapping against your car
        window
tonight. At the Women's Infirmary (now Post Office) they have
        been
screaming, chained, they are screaming their one hundred, two
        hundred lashes
as if silence would not resettle.
What was it? No. That was nothing. You hear nothing.

I **"These subversives, these Friends Of The Dirt"**
Joh Bjelke-Petersen

The Enemies Of The Dirt might dabble
in Real Estate with a nod to the Local Council
but they'd swallow a rainforest before breakfast
and are planning to skillet the Barrier Reef
that is, after the hard work of quarrying
has been dealt with in the telex room.
The Enemies Of The Dirt pride themselves
on their cracked hard-work nails. Their vivid necks
bulge above regulation collars. They know
all the hardships of was it really forty years back?
They do know what bludgers are. The Enemies Of The Dirt
know too well the dirt they grew from (before the subdivision).
From high windows there is a million-dollar view
of the nearly-new freeway that blots out the riverbank
(all those mangroves). Necks creep at the thought of mozzies.
The big floods might still rise to tackle this denuded topsoil
and good luck then to the Friends Of The Dirt, who are under
each arch looking for chinks with soiled khaki shoulderbags
crammed with seeds. Seeds, growth — in this climate?
"Green shoots can split the rock", someone said. No,
someone wrote that: language, another subversive.
"If it moves, shoot: if it doesn't, chop." Up so high,
the Enemies Of The Dirt have an affinity for axes, they sense
the vulnerability of towers, they have a sudden instinct
for Protected Species.

II   "The Joyner Act": A Queensland Text

It is hereby declared, under the Rona Joyner Act
that possession of any book, artefact or item
of printing contrary to Revealed Truth constitutes
an infringement of the Law. Already the libraries
of leading dissident religious bodies (we cite
both Catholic and Anglican Archbishops) have been
confiscated and their possessors placed under bond.
The Coalition Leader (himself a Lay Preacher known
to possess a substantial cache of books) has,
as a special act of clemency by our Premier
and by his direct intervention at Police Headquarters
been pardoned his acts of possession and allowed
to remain in public office (subject, of course,
to participation in the public burning of his books).
The Opposition, by this Legislation, forfeits all rights
and the due processes of Law shall be strictly carried out.
For the benefit of the Community, teachers found
in possession are hereby deprived of certain benefits
(Superannuation, holiday entitlement, Long Service Leave)
at great saving to the Electorate; they have (another example
of legislative clemency) not otherwise been prosecuted.
Yet. They are, for the present, needed to staff schools.
However, a systematic police search of individual libraries
and private holdings of books is being undertaken
as a matter of urgency. The Premier assures his constituents
that the matter of Law and Order will be upheld vigorously.
He is acutely aware of his responsibilities. His Police
have the matter under control. All law abiding citizens
are assured they have nothing to fear.

III   Advice to a Politician

Do not answer questions: ask them.
Do not forget your friends: use them.
Do not forget your enemies: use their mistakes.
Do not forget yourself: if you do, deny it.

Have an Enemy. That is essential.
If you cannot find an Enemy Of The People
find an Enemy Of The Law. Change the Law,
if necessary, to do it (the law has been acquired,
piecemeal, by politicians other than in Queensland).
There is a lot of prejudice waiting to be harvested:
remember — bigotry is only indefensible
when it is apologetic.
Hitler showed the political strength of bigotry,
Mussolini showed the voting power of prejudice.
Learn from them. Of course you do not go so far
as that (of course)
                    Got things done, though;
          the Electorate was contented, dissidents
          could always leave. Trains were on time.

You will find enemies easily enough.

This is a wealthy place, waiting to be exploited.
Are you the one to do it? Slip through an Amendment
to the Companies Act and use nominees. Brazen it out.
And remember: justify nothing.

People who live by the open sewer
    forget it was once a shaded creek.
People who drive the bare road between Bulimba and the
      airport
    forget it was once shade rainforest.
People who live in development brick-veneer bungalows
    have forgotten entirely whatever was once meant by words
    like "community".
You will go far
    taking us all with you.

A record of Flamenco singing

How does a proud man sing
in our culture?
How does an old man sing
his own song here?
How do the sounds coil
out of the throat
how does the throat prepare
to take that offering?
We do not even spit phlegm
here, without embarrassment.

In my country
old men do not sing.
We have closed off
elegy, defiance.
We will not remember
the release possible
the terrible monkeys in the voice
taunting us
haunting
holding out ripe sweet grapes
bitter lemons
in handfulls, till we gulp.

I   A broken tooth

Your teeth, he said, tell more than you'd care to admit.
Your jaw grinds night after night at the mill
you inherited young and believed indestructable.
Time is short — what was the job? Will you do it
now, after all these years? There is this thing about habit
that believes it deals with stone and flint and all
the reassuring surfaces. It deals in surfaces. Tell
that to your teeth, let them grind down the long night
to forget what even rocks cannot forget.
Or let it be said as simple evidence: tonight
you will again begin the writing, the script
proving how ruthless your mouth is and how adept.
"Your mouth", he said, "shapes round your teeth, and your face
round your mouth. At a certain point, to smile is no use."

II   Politics

One of my fingernails turned into a claw
and there's a war against my little toe
— but you don't see that — it hides in my shoe
which I polish hard. I spit on it (so!)
then wipe with old paper: that's what paper's for;
newsprint, letters, phonebook, I know
several laws, lists, agendas I'd like to do.
You, too?

One of my shoes turned into a habit.
One of my feet into a hairless white grub with nails.
I keep wiping, someone told me it works
and look at my shoes, the young don't any more.
Look at one of my shoes. Look at my nails
— no, not this hand. You've not seen
intention calcify as a claw before?

III   Taste

You think my fingers are stained look at my tongue:
you stare at my hands, my fingers are crabs scuttling off
to reach edges and my taste would frighten you. That's if
you got close enough (apologise, child). Crabs clatter among
spoils, imagine the taste their flesh invites — your tongue
moistens, my tongue is as eager still. Of course you laugh,
it's alright. What about taste? Once, would you believe,
hands dried at the feel of an earthworm, they were nervous
        among
the rasping bristles on the stem of wild sunflowers.
Once, too, my tongue stretched like a starched serviette
across tight knees. Knees apologise. No, forget
that, forget the gristle, the body on all fours.
Taste, though. It's about a crab's mandibles among
mangrove juice. You know your own tongue?

IV   On the grass

Alone, you think of that: old men alone
on lawn. So many times your life holds grass
like a smell never forgotten. Those times pass
and you have forgotten. The first one
was taste and explore, you were very sure and began
at the mouth. You were One. Press a few years
onto the bank, streak it with clay, it was
a game of hiding away, stalking, you were on your own.

You tasted stalks, and thought a bit, not about games.
The others were hiding in grass, too. Somewhere you knew.
Later, in love, you rolled the grass soft, I did too.
Cut, forget, sit down again. It always comes
to this — in parks old men, alone. Grass.
They have something to share. They forget this.

V   Doing the old man proud

Doing the old man proud, they say. Doing
the old man. They think I'll say "thanks" today
but I'll bully them for yesterday, I'll clack away
like morse code (remember that?) showing
them I have interest rates still accrueing
in my head (can they add, is their brain dead?) the way
that kept me awake at night from a long day.
Accrueing an old man's pride is what I'm doing.

No pride. Not in that, not now. They do
me proud with visits, most solicitous.
I'm not to be left alone's what it really is.
You call, you visit me, not I visit you.
Well, you can't escape in your own home.
I leave them mess, something to do, when they come.

VI   Old man proud

It's not time to buy clothes
I will wear a suit of linen
It's not time for new things
I see them; I will have 'em
It's not time for time anymore
I will take a holiday
It's not time to be planning for that
I have sailed yesterday

It's time for willing and leaving things
I suppose there will be something over
It's time for handing everything over
It's time I took a lover
You're getting past that, it's time you knew
I'm getting there, just don't rush
You haven't got time, you've swallowed time
Just don't make this linen crush.

VII   Young men's bodies

So out of reach. Yet the wish to reach. What for?
Towards, perhaps. *Perhaps* is what answer?
The only answer is out of reach, perhaps further
than any young body could reach toward. Sure
of itself (that is the condition), let the sweat pour
as if the boy did not even heed his odour
(what for?) (why are you searching?): let the youngster
steer his body simply. Let your jaw

screw tight, then, provide applause. You provide envy.
No, not that, dream you provide lust. Why not
admire the body, muscle, prick and sweat
of the living body, why not? The young man's body
veers, leers (it is himself), draws towards something to learn.
So out of reach. You reach. You did not learn.

VIII   Young girls' bodies

Bodies already, immediate body — to be girls
plots girls into being their hip-sway, body play, target
in the clip-board gallery. Moving, something forgets about
time declared, time off, time of bodies. Girls
are bodies that provoke absence. They stand. A skirt swirls
perhaps, breasts rise with the shoulder, legs invite sweat
or the chafe of rubbing, we dreaming opening the light
already exploring that darkness. This darkness reveals

that we want more. That I want. Darkness. Girls
who know that to open the darkness of legs has no
envy know that darkness is not theirs now although
in the dark they go, grow, make (tell me) something that fills
the taking male ego, swells the possession. In.
So simple. Best words are. Towards. Begin.

IX   Old man's love

I unfold your little titties, girl, back
into the cup of my hands, ignoring the ribs
and their hungry ridges — I hope the horny knobs
of my fingers still invent some hide-and-seek
of feeling thereabouts. Your belly is cool and slack
and pale as my inner leg. But the juice sobs
and glistens inside those lips — that place still keeps
young and secretive and cunning in the dark.

If we close our eyes it is not to imagine boys
and girls with sunlit flanks and shy with each other,
their hunger still confused with pride, their wonder
mixed with lust and anger. We close our eyes
and there is sun on our flanks, yes even our own.
Or it is night, there are stars, wind. We are alone.

X   Old man's newspaper

A page of newsprint is a cage of terrible monkeys
in the voice, they have a habit of mine too well.
I try not to scan headlines, but like a mandril's prick there is
far too much rhetoric. I've been too close
to the cage, they have nothing to show. Snickering, they show
the way to slap meat on a tray, although
the price is up in the stalls. Headlines swallow my peace.

What if I wanted something to drink? My tongue
is a newspaper war, as I've said before. Oh, sure?
I'm not at all sure what the clatter of print is for.
You are on your own, then? Probably. One voice among
many, a crowd, a colony, monkeys picking fleas.
So many words, not looking, looking. All like these.

XI   Two a.m.

What do you want? What I want
is explained as a glass of water,
wine, blood, follow the image
to its source — I want that,
the source. You offer what that
is: I want that to be
what you offer.
                    You want
and are unfulfilled. In the glass
the water does not taste like blood,
the blood not like wine. Against lips
glass smooths out our pressure.
Against glass all liquids make their swirl,
they spill, flow, you want
glass to break. You clench your hand
around glass. You want to drink.

XII   Old man's moment of understanding

There is no silence. That is my understanding
and it's precise. My body is not silence
(it's a kiss and a fart), bodies are without reticence
or decorum often enough. I am longing
for silence, but even God is not having
any of that. At least, not yet. Patience,
you say? The grave is full of noises, digestion
transferring the energy source to whatever's the next thing.

Not even a little silence. Lots of dark
— that's why we sing, curse, clap hands, your hands
on mine sometimes but the dark grins and understands
us alone. The light is God, dark is the back
of God, who turned away in the great God-bed,
dreaming of silence also. There is no silence, He said.

XIII   Old man's fit

I know my own anger, do you own yours?
— the thumb at the neck, the body on all fours,
teeth ground to seacoasts in the jaws
and salt in the eye, a hundred shores
pounded, retreating, pounded because
surf rakes over with combs with claws
and the angers that in old men cause
deep rips to form make gulls scream applause.

Words, you say. The image squints. It draws
me further out of my depth, it pours
me tumbling among shells. Again on all fours
I spit. As I rise I spit phlegm. My jaws
ache to suck further. Are you afraid of that?
The thumb beat pounds again. Applause. Applause.
Applause. Applause.

XIV   Song

Grass ready to burn
was all my childhood was
the old man said.

Grass ready to cut,
to make way for another heading,
and I trampled it myself.

What was it I just said? Those were the years
before I rolled it like a double bed
as I've just said. I talk like grass

when grass is dry, ready to burn.
Ready to harvest — I've done all that;
remember, though, when it's soaked with rain

remember the tang of that, that's what I said.
He turned. Too damp yet. Not
set to burn at all. A lifetime to learn that,
and so much burned already, so much said.

Old Man's Fugue

I
I overlook a zoo: pheasants stalk
among nursery plants in their plastic black

two peacocks swerve behind cane, the gibbons bounce
on their waterbeds of blackboard sound. No fence

holds in the black-beaked ibis, gardeners stoop,
groups of strollers pause and gaze. Stop.

The game is up. Inside or out, a calm
holds everything. The feeling's dangerous. I'm home

and I don't like it. I revel in it, just this once.
Have I missed anything? Next word should be "dance"

but it comes out "pounce". Ostrich hides in a shed,
not the thumped sand. Lizards feign dead.

A boat moved over the water. Cormorants heard,
shoulders showed their listening. A gun and they'd be dead.

On the main road there are a few pelts, a rusty dent,
the whoop of traffic, all at once. Direction of went,

of then or of good as. Pheasants are plucking the song
(it's by Richard Strauss and Eva Braun hummed it). Wrong.

It was an Ode by Purcell to the Music Of War
— a countertenor showing Art what the song is for

but without the gangrene or the sabre-pull. Gibbons shreik
at glissando pitch. Whitman would have understood. To speak

of a shared company is to dissolve the cage.
Zoo noise apes masturbation. Masturbation is rage.

II
Your hair grown long, thick
to be where I recall your arched neck.

If you cut it now, the gone
matting, threshing me with taste, will remain.

III
You know that. In the Japanese art book
Utamaro showed us how sexual is the neck

and how a wad of paper tissues by the bed
offered a whole zoo-full of promises. Said.

IV
A zoo is cages, right? The saved specimens,
the slave species. Man hosing concrete. Fines.

Next word: the ostrich panics, neck thrust,
wings sketching flight, flight a circle, raising dust,

treading the same dust. Is it so far away?
Is it closing in? Closer? False dismay,

safety fence, pheasants stalking among nursery plants.
White pigeons resettle in the peppermint-gum. Ostrich dance.

Again: kangaroos in a group, suddenly off.
What danger? Men driving home. Cage-safe.

V
The gardener knows his seedlings, and is silent enough.
The overalled keeper hosing cages. Voices slip off

even visitors share in this. Nothing to say.
A zoo's silence is not nervous. Bird sound, animal sigh.

Slower and more distant. Each pares from each. Not stretch
but some distance. Distance beyond touch.

VI
How much — words hope to get where we are
but we are not even then, and never there.

It is as if we had to be somewhere
at all times. Here

Something's established. It has not been anywhere near.
Words are the tricks in the mouth, they taste queer.

And we can't be without taste, right? One square.
Taste of hair back of your neck. Flesh sweet-sour.

Admit it: we're caged in the words that free us
from grunt, gimme, mine. Words see us. Words do not see.

VII
A calm. Dangerous. Said from my eighth floor height.
High rise solitudes. No earth to spit.

Remember how the gobbets curl dust around them
in to their moisture-spell? We are brothers in phlegm

if that means something. Drying means something.
The throat cleared goes on expecting that loss again.

Why do I turn all messages to grief?
Why not anger? A good spit — I make it gross, like a thief

compulsively shitting in the agape safe.
Is it all just disposal? Men with pans and shovels move

modestly behind; speciments quick for the test
while still warm. We dream to be rich compost.

VIII
The onlooker at the love ceremony.
Our Japanese prints revive not only memory

but ways. Wise designer, Utamaro, plays
us false, has us. Past as present. Cross over. Pass.

Of course no is yes, that this, guess
already certainty. The onlooker, us,

taking to give back, backing off for wires,
curtain, screen, withholding, holding, is.

Still is. Out of the moment, out of the room,
just that far. A hair still in my mouth. Name.

Word. The thing clutched into, clutched, watched
in its very moment of no-word. The word wished

then, known to be there, somewhere. Fought for
(the deaths for). Onlooker. The ceremony came here

into this room, we can still see it, that is the word.
As much there as anywhere. As such witnessed as said.

IX
The lions in the zoo roar, mate and wait
to play the keeper at their feeding gate.

My lovers stay up late (all night)
and greet me heavy-eyed but straight.

They heard the caged things copulate at four a.m.;
at five they grinned as gibbons stripped to climb

the blackboard squeal of mating round
the corners of their hosed compound

(they heard kitchens of birds demand the sun
beaks ripping up scales, gulping them down,

and the paper-comb of Norfolk Pines ready to tongue
the rough salt out of the needling song)

they heard at six the cloudy elephant resume
its clock-wise pendulum

and palm-squirrels (they heard them) free
as they'll ever be. My lovers heard

the peahen's absurd
word for or against her trampling lord.

They drifted on their absurd bed
as if they brought what they had dreamed inside

as if their flesh were petal smooth
(it is) their youth

(it is) were shared. My lovers greet me in my zoo.
They expose their share of each other. I can go.

X
Old men on a top floor are allowed to crow,
dance, piss, dribble, lean over balconies, to

stare, smoke their lungs to tar, coffee, pulp.
All that's on top floors let them enjoy. A yelp

like blackboards rubbing (remember?) out of the zoo.
Who? When? Piston-slap of thighs rubbing *who*?

sweat out of pores of the neck, hair matting *who*?
the small shoulders, the skin, fingers roving, *you*

spying, sharing, fingers believing in words, *you*
sounds got out, escaping, *you*, slap of bodies, *you*

looking on, before meaning, *who who*, entering, *who*
twist on the bed, the sprout, leaf, pod, *who*

yourself, myself, onlooker, inlooker, who
of us, *who*, the voice dragging darkness, even the zoo

(the gibbons), 'leon' shreiks a peacock, *you you*
nothing slow, who believes slow, nothing me or you

outside to be outside to, outside, make nothing to make
do, make and be, being nothing, for the sake

of nothing, anything, straws in a wind, in your fingers
held tight in your hand (sweating) clutching, *who*, angers

clutching through, on a top floor, in an old man's words
that are your turn, me and you, the code understood, seedpods

bursting not withholding. Sharing. Remembering.
That's more than words, that's *beginning*

Who said that? On a top floor, the onlooker at cages
pulls the curtain. Wires tug sound out of distances.

A boat moved over the water. Cormorants were listening,
their shoulders bobbed together, throats agape, glistening.

Your hair so long. Neck. A wad of Utamaro tissues.
Next word. Now? Who? The celebration praises **you**.

The glass vase

The thing made scoops up more than glass and ashes,
time and a bit of ingenious craft. The thing
drags place inside from time as if to bring
secrets along with it — so that it reaches
us always. It is not immortal (our wishes
are never for so improbable and rigid a thing).
In the moods of light all things alter. We sing
out of time in our time: the heart quickens, throat catches.

I bring you this glass vase because it can break —
the bronze rim of leaf and locust-grip
mottles the shaft as sensitively as a lip.
That classifies part: Paris, Art Nouveau. Take
it up in your hands, place it in this light.
We are there — not place, not time: immediate.

Motel Amalienburg

I
The housemaids must boggle: you bring your typewriter,
three framed prints (2 for me!), cassettes, books,
catalogues, a silver dinosaur, a special vase
— across benches and beds we strew our visible accomplices
as if we were a barricade, holed in for the seige.
We draw the blinds,
we tear at each other's clothes, they are part
of the wilful clutter. At dusk we sip cognac
and then saunter out
ready for anything.

II
In the botanical gardens we walk slowly.
I rattle off names of trees, sometimes accurate.
I point out Tristania Alberta, acclimatised
native of Brisbane. Brown water. Grassslopes
damp the way we recognize. We walk so slow,
naming things, storing in our way as they in theirs.
You call for an icecream. Yes, that too.

III
It is years since I soaped another's back.

IV

5 p.m. and we're out of cash. We dine in
on ryebread and leftover cheeses. We have built
archives into any corner store and a gallery
into this motel. What is its name? Let's call it
The Amalienburg. Let's invent the Rococo together.
Let's invent landscapes and terraces — and a pond,
there must be a brown pond and a swan. Black? White?
We have the choice, now. No matter what god
scheduled them, they're ours. Let's return, let's
forget them all, let's invent each other's body.

The Ceduna Amalienburg Motel

Braille midnight, our fingers are hungry readers and the
text is on a parchment that turns till we gasp with eagerness.
Chapter's end. The book hardly absorbed, but fingers relax,
uncurl, or curl like petals to dark clusters, flower-clusters
still warm against the warm side of the wall, all the time
in the world.
The body of midnight repeats 26 letters of discovery, the
7 acts. Language is out already into the garden, alone now,
sure of midsummer fragrance, sure of response to fragrance,
skilled as braille fingers at reading what is abundant
at this hour. The midnight garden allows night full entry
into afterglow, into its walls.

Eyes closed, we scan
fingertips
as if they were
bodies, bodies
as if they
were
fingers reaching
with eyes
closed
opening.

Motel room. Cavity brick neighbours, a stain on the carpet
where I did spill some wine, one shoe near the door the other
with two socks stuffed, how did your leather jacket get there
how did my tourist guide get under your good skirt

                                                    we did not
drink a bottle of wine   and before eating   we did
open the gate into the Amalienburg garden, our rococo pasture
nobody knows is on the maps because it is written in braille
and in private
                        bricks still warm from the sun   the flowers knew
the stars a braille script of our choice   we laugh
at puzzled faces, the travelling salesman, the bickering family
stars inside our wall, sun inside, we are inside right inside
the serrations and pricks of braille
language lets us go we are there

Oceans

Those who live sea-edge are sifters and collectors.
If you live inland, do you recognize fossils
    unearthed in your backyard, or in the Mains excavation?

Those used to walking the sea edge with nothing to do
    have always something to look for.
Inland, you read of the whale as a specimen bound to
    extinction.
    Has it a right to live?

Those scuffling across sandhills, reaching last night's tideline,
    looking at water and the mobility we know has a salt task
    through ninety-percent of our own body, need to have seen
    whales
    only once, passing,
though they may not, returning inland, be precise in explaining
    exactly why they remember.

The great whales lollop in dream continents, submarine, beyond
    subdivision. There has grown wonder in dry bones. We
    have needs we are sure about. There are moments we feel,
    in our ears, amphibian.

Those who have seen visions

Those who have seen visions do not smile.
They speak. They take a ripe peach and bite
straight through the furzy skin to the juice. They shit
as the body directs. They have seen visions while
at just such functional tasks. You cannot tell
and yet you tell at once. Is it an absence of light
or a presence? It is a burden. Even the night
cannot ease knowledge. There is no escape at all.

On an obscure wall with quick strokes on wet plaster
Piero della Francesca painted Christ
lifting his heavy torso, released at last
into vision. The painter was concentrating his cluster
of geometric tokens to clamp like a bite
against the neck of absence. We flinch alright.

The Elegy Fires

The old woman does not tell the nurse
but she has had to reach out
to touch the flames upon her wardrobe.
The wood is uncharred. Around the bed, too,
flames. And last night a hand
beside her own. Eyesight failing,
and the ghost fires, she stared again
to make sure — the hand of her own mother.

With her own unfamiliar hands, lost
for words, she begins the letter
to her son and the date she writes
is ten years out. Ten years, burnt out
as if they had never mottled her
and no ash. Ten years,
ten leaves out of a diary
and her palms are the colour of old newsprint.
"Why do you never write?" one page,
one line of script, ten years, forty years.

Abridgements, she made her virtue out of discarding things.
The bookcase to one daughter, the Doulton to another.
She rid herself of a lifetime's possessions. Her children
have weathered, squinting faces, ash-grey hair.
In the unconsuming fire what may return in a vortex?
        Two children
splashing, green woollen bathers hugging into the creases.
Even the sudden gust of shoreline seaweed that made her hurry
        them on
to somewhere cleaner, how could that come back? Each grain
in her ocean-damp sandshoes bound again, knotted tight,
as if she still had young feet.

Where is the nurse? She has let go everything
but the ring on her strong, useless, mottled hand.
The bitter arguments of those middle years have been let go,
the long sea-trip back home with little Grace
when she had to discover finally there was nothing left
in Andover. The fretting over money. Parched summers
year after year. Not all things return.
The flames caress her hands
they hover round her body as if she had no body.
This is not her body, this parody crumpled under sheets.
Flames without heat. Years of purpose drawn up,
hours of waiting.
Hours of work in kitchens, committees,
minutes alone with dew speaking down by the fowl-run,
      minutes.
She stares for focus, she will outstare flames.
Focus is difficult now, rainbow. She is betrayed
as once in childhood she was mocked
by a fractured spectrum.

Is this memory? Out loud her voice is a phone-call,
close but cupped in. "What parts of our brain function
to achieve this? I know the flames are hallucination."
No, she will not disturb the nurses.
The flames are visible. The hand of her mother
is visible. She knows, soon, there will be the voices.

Fifty years since her mother whispered. Things that come back
to choose her are not of her deciding. Must she now
endure everything?
Her son, who came this morning, has not returned
for ten years, forty years. That person is not her daughter.
Updraught. If only her mother's hand were comforting:
it is another claimant. If you do not give
it shall be taken. What you give away
shall return a thousandfold.

Italy

I
I remember in Naples
the vendor of lemons
who crushed the ripe fruit
across cool ice.
I remember his arms
like harvest orchards
where shoulders are bare
to reach up high
for the furthest fruit
and tongue discovers
that sweat is a lick
of lemon rind.
Remembering that flavour
I wipe my mouth
with the back of a hand.

II
To eat a peach first bring a glass bowl
into the room and place a selection of fruit
carefully: do not bruise. You must get
cold water — one imagines a mountain pool
but kitchen faucets have their convenience. Fill
to a nice balance. Fruit seem to sweat
with air globules, but these slowly let
go. Place your bowl on the table.

Dipping fingers quickly, make your choice —
not like the French, squeezing and testing, but by sight.
It is assumed, in the country, that every peach can not
be perfect, it is a close approximate. When you pass
the bowl to your neighbour, you take your knife, then cut.
What are you thinking? Why are your eyes shut?

Copyist in the Louvre

Planes. Volume. Texture. Surface.
A step-by-step process, patently. Patiently, I recreate
the lips, smile, glow on the still-delicate cheeks
of the Dowager-Princess: you learn,
copying. Like a queue for taxis, onlookers lose identity
behind me. Some interrupt. It is a sort of wit
to show them my concentration.
Georgio, who endlessly repeats the Franz Hals, must explain
in detail, making his work a little theatre. Six copies
this month, and he has sold them all.
The Dowager-Princess stares back at me, glow
of the last warm summers. I think I have fallen in love.
No sales. To copy better than Georgio is not enough:
I despise his smiles, banter, play-actions.
Why am I always making lists? Georgio, Jules, Ishimo,
Vincent, Romain, Stanley the American — there are lists
for each bone within my hand, every muscle and sinew
is enumerated, every thing I have is a copy.
The part that is myself is very small: they say
we are simply energy expressed in a particular concentration;
like fingerprints, different yet hardly distinguishable.
I make my own image in this meticulous copy
by the laying on of brushstrokes. There are names for copyists.
The Dowager, of course, would have scorned me. All her
          sittings
would have delighted the Salon: music, conversation,
portraitist discreet yet conscious of his jest with
          immortality.
Later: "Yes, ah, that summer . . . ", or "Remember me
     then . . . "

Or simply an instruction to remove the painting. I
transcribe scrupulously. I do not have to consider
possibilities beyond surface, volume, texture. I hate Georgio,
he is so slipshod, so inaccurate. When he turns
as he always does, he grins at me, delighted —
with his work, with a sale, with the way light
suddenly changes through the window. The flush of pleasure
in his cheeks. Momentary. Unforgettable.
If I were an artist truly, I would paint him.

The silver rose

The secret is not to look at models or diagrams.
Each rose has its own imperfection. Begin from that.
Commission: one silver rose, with concealed perfume cache.
You have to endure each petal till the silver believes
it can unfurl from the same command that hardens the thorn.
Hours, weeks, spent in the Jardin des plantes
to catch the thrust of the bud discarding the sheath
and I still brace as the petal arm crumples to unfold.
But it is necessary to observe
till the bloom sags, bulges
into leather: revelation of the corolla
and the surprising seed.

Metal shines in a wealthy man's eye, his lady
fingers the bauble. I grow by their unseriousness.
I grow by things I make. This rose
will cost you the earth. No, I said
look closer. The earth: you would suppose
my toy dipped in silver
and still alive.

This garden withholds its curse, yes I know that.
Every plant I stole, dreamed of in silver, made
into the reflection we all are caught by into surprise.
The homage of imperfection, the terrible homage
of perfect mimickry.
                              Roses mocked me. Silver
is thing, an object — the Spaniards were simple
but not foolish to smelt it to dull bricks.
Craft is artifice. No, the artifice is in me.
I have not discovered what I have discovered:
only that there is an ache in the rose, in my copy,
that becomes reliquary. Rose petals scatter before me
easily, unvaluable. A thick shadow stoops down
with gross fingers. They are my own.

Richard Wagner at Schloss Donndorf
Beyreuth, 1873

The porcelain stove is not efficient.
It is too efficient, it dries me out. It drives me out
into the park: some first leaves striking
the mirror of autumn, cupped hands around a stove,
golden yet disconsolate. There should be light and warmth,
if only in my bones. This morning the smell of linden,
blossoms littering their scurf and frangrance
tickled me up, Cosima says. I detest spring,
I hate more the last days of linden summer,
stiffening finger-pods under wasted seed.
I'm sick of playing Bach in E Flat Minor. I'm
sick of being in love, of falling, of falling out
of overheated rooms in search of search (children
were outside last night, why?). This park's imposture.
I do not believe in the lake; I ache at the edge, leaning
on the rustic bridge. I think I will dream the Rhine in flood,
pillars of flame, Gods in our petty squabbles searching us,
aching into our very bones. I think I will dream linden forests
as a prayer — what prayer? The prayer for a god
stares at the myth that believes the power of music
can ever ease this scald of seeing one first leaf
repeat autumn's search. The prayer sees gold
stain all green things bound into the rot of air.

This is the richest summer I have ever known.

Inside, there will be coffee, warmed clothes, anxious looks
again — the larger my theatre, the more visible (you'd believe
they would see) the burn of loneliness within. My axe
will strike each linden within the seed.
I'll bring the whole world down, within an orchestral song
that is learning never to come to a point of repose —
my design will power such a conflagration it will take
sixty years to achieve. My theme: the loneliness of one
who finds the porcelain stove too drying, too uncertain,
too certain too hot too cold. My theme: the loneliness
of one defying autumn in the planned garden. My theme:
one who has planted gardens to transfigure your world,
who has opened a prospect here, landscaped a glade.
Theme: power.
Theme: one who is crowded by devotion
into the shade of beech trees, linden. A stove
that is not efficient, a heart likewise, an anger
at leaves, loves, loveliness. An anger, always,
at the unspoken presence of fire, even in damp.

Conrad Martens in 1859

I
Last night (it was last night?) I woke to the lurch
of decking somewhere in Moreton Bay: no,
I was on the *Beagle* again, joking with Darwin;
who is no ape but a lion in London now, I must
tell him that. Shaggy-grey too; more deliberate.
And Wickham, up on the splintery wharf at Brisbane;
no wonder the *Beagle* persists. Ah, old shipmate,
didn't we laugh and slap hands together. Later:
nothing to say. The stoop, I hadn't expected that.

II
"Who are the merchants? There must be officers with an eye
for watercolours to send Home?" I tell my friend, who eyed me
for hints of South America and us both younger, sappy men.
His Magistrate silence. "Moreton Bay has possibilities.
You are here for a beginning — something rich
in the genesis of a settlement, eh?" I go on.
"We are all, you know Wickham, investors in some manner."
He grunts. Lianas and native pines (that shade of denseness,
that tuftiness) isolate the riverbank, the stream curves
many times upon itself like no other river yet remains
generous (how to suggest that?). "It's at night." he warns.
A way of pausing mid-sentence. He spits at a boy.

III
"Well, old shipmate, I suppose you don't laugh at nonsense now
as you used to in the *Beagle* or rather I suppose nonsense
does not come your way. I've set down here in prosperous
          Sydney,
a complacent paterfamilias with lessons and commissions.
Landscape's the thing. Those nights on deck ribbing each other.
I'm afraid of your eloquence. Who'd imagine you, Darwin,
          thinking
beyond parodies, me comfortable in the rough frontier?
Enjoy your fame, dear friend, it's almost as if you,
back in your study, were mapping unknowable frontiers
while I hike (clumsily enough) to fill frontiers
with reassurances that what we see can still be reconciled
with a safe past. Enough. A jolly cruize. We had a jolly life."

IV
Early morning light, the only probable moment —
otherwise as well attempt to portray sweat, heat,
itching.

V
Notes from a diary — at fifty I was still something of a boy:
"25.11.1851: a roomfull of Selectors last night. Ipswich
pre-empts Brisbane (The North Australian Club). Learned
more than a week with Wickham: Handcock ebullient —
          "Ipswich
pushes ahead, will yet be the downfall of Paris". They plot
to return the Convict system, workers at cheap rates. Rev. Lang
opposes ("Inhumane"). I will carry their petitions
to remoter Stations; Art gives me immunity, I feel a southern
Rubens. A few sketches (river, the new wharves) already
promised."   Notes. With a roomful of landowners,
convicts at cheap rates seemed plausible, it was a time
of some economic pressure . . .

VI

Someone told me old Oxley's comments on the Moreton Bay
        tribe.
I respect his eye, the colonial maps will be more than abstracts
of geography. He applauded certain marvels these savages
        achieved
in technology. Instance: river fishing-nets 3 times longer,
much stronger than anything known. Our pride is humbled
in that acknowledgment. The fine stringwork of their woven
        bags.
These specimens hereabouts (they'd steal with their very toes)
mock our attempts to cast them into noble innocence.
        Something
is missing. We are desperate to have them gone.

VII

Australia, you are a rising child, and doubtless
someday will reign a great princess in the South;
but you are too great and ambitious for affection,
and not great enough for respect: Darwin.
                                Dear friend,
your words select a taste of sour
in my choice, as if to accuse.
I had not thought myself so entirely
abandoned.

VIII

If I go to sleep again
I will be somewhere else,
a boy fretting for water,
sail, journeys. Old dark men
turn aside, etched in charcoal.
They spit, itching.

IX
I am sitting now at a rough cedar desk
watching candlelight. Mosquitoes draw blood,
they paint it on my exposed parts
like convict artists, brutalized. Heat
rots my clothing. Wickham spitting at
"our prison February". A pile
of sketches recalling Moreton Bay. I itch.
In the foreground of this watercolour
I will add a ship, the *Beagle*. Night
is brutalized colour: indigo. Brown
nocturnal fruitbats. I cannot imagine
what selection the future will make
from attitudes that have been my own.
They have plans: *the New Athens,*
they plot landscape as money, banknote
pastures. They propose no memories.
What interest will the future pay?

X
I cannot concern myself with responsibilities.
The candle dissolves a lake of singed moths.
My colouring box? money belt? letters
of introduction? No reassurance, the past
squints gap-mouthed. If I go to sleep again
it will be somewhere else. Why am I still anxious,
who is the fretting boy inside? Who spits?
That excellent man, Wickham, such a responsible fellow
and the admirable commonsense of his house at Newstead.
The *Beagle* has floated a long way off.
What possibilities have I abandoned? Somehow
I had not expected Wickham to envy me. I envy him.

At Montalcino, Italy

Anywhere we go to we make change for us.
We make the sky change for us
we make the shadows under trees change
we organize thickets of summer dogrose, we cause traffic
to stop while we plunder wildflowers.
We change everything into ourselves
we change into ourselves as soon as we recognize.
Remember the affront of the airport, tactics
at the bivio? We change everything and we know
everything, often even before we know.
                                        That serpent
just as we turned downhill from the hot park
where a few young boys with pushbikes and insolent exposure
moved just at the last moment in front of us,
that serpent just as we turned beyond the two venerable
      churches
with facades, porticos, museum fragments.
That serpent could be a new message, something we did not
      know.
We strode on without stopping.
The nervous laugh changed to joking on one phrase
and we changed the snake the summer the teasing boys
into that colourful laugh. Reassurance sits on us
like clothing. By this, we claim to have been
to Montalcino.

Learning the French

Before you move into the language you move away.
Before you listen to it, you are hearing words
isolated like a broken string of beads.
These scatter as you pick them up. They play
distinctly snide games to embarrass you. Dismay
is your first lesson. Your second: language needs
growth to grow comfortable in. Start with numbers. Good.
Soon you will answer back, soon you will make
your request without pointing in the charcuterie. Begin
to think beyond weather or money crises in the Métro.
Begin to memorize a few witticisms. No,
you have to be prepared to listen. The throw-off is thin
as a barb of thorn. Learn that. Again you falter.
Having caught the tone, what else can be the matter?

Nimrud Palace Room, British Museum

"Ah, that now, look at it now. That
is the Tree Of Life, you see it? There's
the King: look, even larger than the Tree.
And on the other side, some Deity
we don't know about."

His girth stretches the summer shirt like netting,
his voice enjoys tomb resonance. Grandly, he snubs
the Pakistani attendant. His wife fingers
the Museum Guide with sun-deprived tendrils.
Words illumine.
Yet listeners, eager for discovery, evade him. His
is the most valuable regional library
he explains, too loudly. Under the wide cloth,
pale bare toes. "Imagine that hunting freize
from your throne. No soft textiles there:
hard power." The smell of lions, caged princes,
the King's stench, in the nostrils
like salt shoved up: *Banquet! Royal Prisoners
to bear platters!*
                    "The lot's a lie,
you know. That battle was lost, not won."
He has listened. Penned lions in his library
smother excitement, the King gazes
beyond the Life Tree tendrils at some Deity
he doesn't know: hard power. His wife is thinking
of tea and pork-pie. He gulps at food, he roars
at hostages, and is never satisfied.

"The Champion" Pub, Bayswater Road

She sits in a padded seat in the main bar till closing time.
No one buys her a drink.
She knows that when they all crowd out onto the pavement
someone will proposition her.
She never accepts money.
She prefers to go with them but sometimes she will bring
a young man to her own room.
He is usually shy, it is his first time —
down from the country, or from Scotland
with pink cheeks and very red lips.
She can be gentle but as often as not is indifferent.
He closes his eyes and is enlarged
he explodes into the molecular secrets
of the constructing universe   is raised
and then humbled.
She smokes a cigarette.
There is nothing else to do.
Dressing, he notices the narrow male shape of her shanks
and staggers out wondering. He will have been quite drunk.
Nothing. The cigarette stubs are clawed red with lipstick.
She has forgotten if it had ever been otherwise.
There is today
and there will be tonight again.
She remembers nothing, nobody. The great industry of the
          firmament
engages above her. The breeze comes fragrant
across the fecundity of the park. Endless fecundity,
endless infestation. There are hungers. There are needs.
There is indifference.

Black Widow Spider

"Sometimes I let her out. Crawl
over my arm. If you're not frightened
it is no problem."   He passes
the plastic pill-container around.
Three flies webbed as with meat-hooks.
His spider clings to the white cap.

When forced, she adopts the boxing stance
uneasily and with nervous messages
but the ritual is for keeps, inside
clear plastic.

He lifts his chin, daring the other kids
to demand: "Let her out, then." He tilts
the scar at the left of his eye. He
lifts his chin again, the gym pose.
Then he grins. All the gold of his moustache
binds that smile into suntaut webs.
Five youngsters pass over the trapped spider.
He draws up their edginess like fluid.
They are sucked in.

THREE PARIS PARKS
for Rosemary Wighton

I   In the Parc de L'Ile Saint Louis

The best way to describe shade
        is to remember the burn of sun
        on your forehead.
The best way to describe the green
        of plane-leaves
        is to remember bare winter
        letting scissors of cold cut the wind
        into profiles.
The best way to record the sun's many tangents
        is to imagine photographed leaves
        without movement.

In this park like the prow of a boat
dividing the Seine
it is possible to believe
you are floating.
That is the best way. Now
look at the ground underfoot.
Look at the ceaseless hopping
and scavanging of pigeons.
Think of stillness.
Think of a park in the centre of Paris.
We are ourselves opposites.
We are reconciled.

II Jardin des plantes

The old man empties his pockets — behold, bread.
Sparrows, blackbirds, wood doves, pigeons
even thrushes.
He plays with them, into the coffers of his grip
— not under the grand and terribly pruned formal avenue
but here, near the menageries,
this caged hillock of forest
where spring wildflowers become weeds.
Children in school groups know this old man,
bird man, proprietor of twitterings and cute squabbles.
The teachers order close file, unsure of the danger.
He is sometimes photographed. He does not mind.
He talks to nobody, though his grin is a handclasp.
Some men have found books, some drink themselves blank
in front of their wives. He has a way of being himself
(not as his wife, alive, would have wished).
He has a way of seeming to control birds
and this corner of shadiness.
The teachers are right to fear him, of course.
The children are right to marvel.
He has his rights, of course, he has his silences,
his bonds, his stress, still. That is to be still living.

III   Outdoor sculpture
Tuileries gardens: Henry Moore exhibition

The shapes are giant, but eroded like dead meteors,
debris from satellites.
Step closer, though, there are marks and abrasions
surfaces aching to be fondled
rolled in the hand of some naked giant.
The chestnuts throw tributes of tiny petals
dregs of pollen.
They have leaves of a thousand fingers
hands of the old tree gods.
A pigeon glides to the surface of one of the statues
it pecks as if this were some huge grain
then flies back with perfect dignity.
A man walks under the droppings of that tree
and puts his hand to the statue.

> We know the feel of trees —
> they are growing, as we are,
> drawing up, discarding.
> The tree gods know fertility involves death.

We make our memorials in stone.

It is not that we will be survived by the hard things
it is that we must be reminded of the soft parts of our hands
as a boy carries marbles.

The man moves away from the giant form
thinking of the desire in circles
thinking of the curves in the body
remembering the moon
and how rocks kneel down
without movement
but with secret signs
of some large process.

I   First class

In the Louvre he goes directly to the portrait statue
of Tutankahmen
to examine the erased heiroglyph of the boy King's name
at the back and lower right side of the figure.
In Amsterdam he calculates the waiter's tip
as a precise percentage of the bill
and in Paris he conveys a specific *don* to the chef
because of the asperges.
When he travels alone he shares his taxi from the airport
with the young widow and her two children —
they have dinner together that evening, the tots
left safely (his gesture) with the resident sitter.
He discusses philosophy with the student
sharing his compartment in the Rembrandt express to München
and is careful to quote (in translation) Foucault.
He goes straight to the most discreetly comfortable hotel.
When he retires for the night
he knows exactly what he will do tomorrow
— though there is always room for the unexpected.

II   Second class

The immediate gull, vendors spot him at three hundred metres.
The street photographer at the Opéra will con him
into five underdeveloped polaroid shots: the sheepish expression
immediately recognizable.
In the museum restaurant the girl at the self-serve payout
will scrutineer his too indulgent pile of glazed hors d'oeuvres
and add a tip for herself in the total.
Shopkeepers stand at their doorways to grin him inside;
the price of fruit goes up in the stalls,
there is a shortage of cheap hotels so he ends up in the
        SPLENDIDE
where the doorman scornfully accepts his overlarge tip
and he finds himself in a back room with no bath.
In lounges and through windows he sees others:
relaxed, gracious, animated.
He sits alone, gulps his meal (something he knows; or
        hamburger).
He has done all the tourist spots from the brochure.
He has nowhere else to go.

III   Third class

Was told "don't let them beat you down"
and has now walked many miles burdened with his pack
(labelled with flag and an agenda of stickers)
though the local tram service would have cost less
than a Saturday morning ice cream
and have saved a whole day's exhaustion.
He slept through Amsterdam in Central Station Reservations.
He claims to know Rome (two streets and a pensione);
he did the Louvre, elbowing tourist-busloads,
though he ticked off the same three house specialities
(and bought postcards). How appalling
to stagger, lost, into the Royal Bedchamber
when you were searching for the loo.
A friend told him of a cheap hotel at S. Lazare
so he now has a necklace of bug-bites.
He spits at guided tours and ferries
but has a suspicion he misses out on things.
In London, he made direct for Picadilly Eros.
It was boarded up. The feeling of loss was intangible
but enormous: so much for posters.
Losses: his camera in Rome, his passport in Venice,
his innocence everywhere and nowhere.
When he returns home
he will still have enough in the bank
for a deposit on a second hand Holden.

The journey by bus

When I boarded the B7 for the Cloisters and 195th Street
I did not notice my neighbour was Death.
I got on at 42nd (yes, my exact age). Three people
came into focus: the blind beggar, unheeded;
the well-dressed man queueing for lewd flicks,
and the rejected whore "Ain't I good enough?"
These things, at forty-two, twist attention.

I recall intolerable heat. If it were merely
the forty-second hangover. Sharp nettles at my wrist,
a cold surprising hand pumping under my ribs
massaging quicker, quicker. Because my eyes became
a white sheet stripped on some cold bed
I did not recognize Death. Not until sweat
burst stored wine vats of panic and I almost wept.
My neck ached with grip of pure bone.

Death playing games. Opening my eyes.
Able to open my eyes I looked across Central Park
to three boys playing. They were alive.
The first jerked his frisby high, a shout.
The second dragged a scooter from the third
who taunted, picking his nose and eating.
My arm, I realized, had lost sensation. Then it was raked
like the dead leaves. Death piling the wind fires.

That was when I became aware of the bus, and myself,
travelling. I shivered, sweated in a swoon to remain alive.
I prised my eyes. Another stop. Blurred figures alighting —
an old man leaned against his woman who plucked lice
from her daughter's hair, a thing in bright red.
I swear I saw them. Lips thick carmine. Judgment.
I reached out with my tongue, my lips were not dead roseleaves.
Wires of pain were intent on reconnecting me.
"Well, all out here" the conductor leaned back, "This is it,
      baby."

Trump Street

The second death of Lazarus:
no one says how long after the first
but we can surmise no extended period,
the miracle being confirmed.
Think of his breath: no sweet herb
will console him, ever.
About him, always flies, something
clinging.

Or is it true there is only the one death —
that cursed he shambles still, a skeletal beggar
you step from turning the corner out of Trump street;
the one who does not ask, does not shuffle a claw
or a withered child for coins, who hugs with endurance
the burden of that curious proof once made
(like a sleight of hand) by the gentle man
who turned, then, about his other business
of healing, comforting, laying on of hands?

A party under the Weeping-Fig
for Helen Haenke, in memory.

I
The year's ending — appropriately, in our country,
that means summer, full-pelt, full sunlight pelting
us down or up or out of doors. We heap the year's end
with accumulating sunshine and the best flowers still
grow solicitous for a future, heaping the past into growth.
Summer is trampling the past, trampling us almost
while this all happens. The weeping-fig, though,
spreads over us, outside seasons, evergreen,
its shade
a refuge.

II
When you wrote to me you were dying
I was in Tuscany, full summer of June. I took your letter
out into the olive grove, careful for vipers. The shepherdess,
Nella, in her late 70s, was scything down red poppy flowers
among stalks of drying grass. Malva flowers were weeds, simply
Camomile pushed out gold-puffy cheeks, yes, that sort of
                              impudence.
Seemingly immortal. Summer. Full European summer
and very far away from almost everything.
It slid on, it was growing on my return here,
summer, building up, counting down, waiting,
scythe-strokes of an impersonal shepherdess.

III
We are afraid of death.
We do not know the language of it.
We back off.
You were given a fixed appointment
— not chance, not excess and adventure.
You were given complete countdown.
Counting
began.
We
were
afraid.
We were fumbling with numbers.
You looked at us,
counting. Language looks backward,
it does not count; it records,
it remembers.

IV
The loneliness of dying
is the first journey truly alone.
We are born surrounded
we claim flesh more than our own from the start.
We make flesh, more than our own, we own flesh
other than our own. Even alone, we are flesh
sharing a known understanding with flesh,
with the sharing bond of senses.
The growth of sharing surrounds us. One thing,
only, is alone.

V
We are not, by nature, deciduous.
Helen, you understand this,
and smile at me.
At the end, it is not that we die
but the way
the passage requires our dying.
As if we were still
in process,
as if we were unfinished,
not still,
as if we were
unfinishing,
leaves of an evergreen.
of this weeping-fig.

VI
When the first guests arrived you were there
when the conversation was an awkward side-glance you were
        there
when someone greeted an old friend you were there
and strangers being introduced knew you were there too.
You were there as someone fingered a leaf, evergreen,
as someone remembered wild poppies.
You were there as eyes sought out dark bloodmarks on croton
        leaves,
you were there as fingers carefully stroked the glass-stem
when champagne was poured.

Someone laughed suddenly. You were there.
Someone laughed too loud. There, smiling
in the words, there out of the words, showing us
the shady area beneath the fig
sharing it.
You were there as we searched for words,
as we became, in being there, your reflections,
part of something beyond our own bucking selves.
You were smiling at us then, meeting the many layers
of your being in each other's reflection.
The garden was part of you, part of the reflection
we were part of. We moved inside
knowing it would be there a long time. We went on with the
          party
inside. You were free to go.
You have left before us, knowing
it was a success.

His first real snow

I
3 p.m. dark.
Trees are burnt banknotes,
streetlights wince
as if coins were flung.
Uphill, you are nobody.
Downhill
you turn a corner, clutch
imbalance. There is blood
on the snow, frozen.

II
A black-green statue in snow wind.
In snow shadows the boy's naked buttocks
grow elderly, drawn in. Next week,
perhaps skeletal.

III
That blood spatter, was it
entirely red, do I forget
or imagine? I imagine
snow covers things
I imagine walking out
abandoning prints, I imagine
how sheets of paper catch up in air,
snow spiral. I imagine the bronze boy
two dimension, one dimension, snowdrift.

IV
Snow is a company of many shareholders.
To vote, you must first sign.
To sign, you must first open your hand.
To open your hand you must first
make it naked.
To make it naked you must test it.
To test it you must draw blood.
It was your own blood
in the snow.
Welcome.